Contents

Dedication

I would like to dedicate this book to my husband Paul and son Liam for their
continued support, understanding and patience during my creative journey.

My family and friends for their moral support.

A big thank you to all those in the craft trade whose contributions made
this book possible.

F.R.

This edition published in 2005 by Search Press Ltd, Wellwood, North Farm Road, Tunbridge Wells, Kent, TN2 3DR

First published in 2003 by The Crafthouse Press Limited, Design House, 49 High Street, Pershore, Worcestershire

Text copyright © Françoise Read 2003, Photography copyright © The Crafthouse Press 2003

All rights reserved. No part of this book, text, photographs or illustrations may be reproduced or transmitted in any form or by any means by print, photoprint, microfilm, microfiche, photocopier, internet or in any way known or as yet unknown, or stored in a retrieval system, without written permission obtained beforehand from Search Press.

ISBN 1 84448 119 0

The publishers and author can accept no responsibility for any consequences arising from the infomation, advice, or instructions given in this publication.

Readers are permitted to reproduce any of the items in this book for their personal use, or for the purposes of selling for charity, free of charge and without the prior permission of the Publishers. Any use of the items for commercial purposes is not permitted without the prior permission of the Publishers.

Printed in Malaysia by Times Offset (M) Sdn Bhd

Introduction

All stampers have a thirst for inspiration, myself included! While doing workshops and demonstrations I am always amazed and delighted by the response to new ideas. So when I was asked to write a book I knew exactly what I wanted to put forward… lots of ideas. Contained within the book are 25 projects to stimulate those creative juices. Many techniques, materials and styles are covered that will inspire you to use the huge selection of stamps that are now available.

By completing the projects you will gain experience in all areas of stamping. There are plenty of books, videos and workshops available to teach the basic skills. This book goes one step beyond and is aimed at helping you to develop. Each project has a certain look achieved by using a group of related images and one or more techniques and stamping styles. I have used lots of different colour schemes, materials and surfaces, so you should gain plenty of experience in how to create, mount and present a wide variety of cards. There are plenty of ideas on adding finishing touches too. A complete materials list and step-by-step instructions are provided with each project so that you can duplicate the finished cards. Along the way there are tips to help you or to suggest alternatives. Many of the project have different

cards, produced in the same style, to give you further ideas to try.

Above all, try to use the projects as springboards for exploring your own ideas and developing your own style, adapting them to the stamps already in your collection. There are many occasions when you want to send a special greeting card and all the cards created in this book can be used or adapted for all kinds of celebrations.

Techniques

Here are some of the techniques used in the projects:

Enamelling
Stamping into a hot thick layer of embossing powder or glazing over an image with a thick layer of embossing powder.

Shrink Plastic
Stamping on a sheet of shrink plastic, cutting out the image, heating and shrinking the image.

Sponging
Applying ink to the surface of the card with a sponge. A stencil or paper mask can be used in the process.

About the Author

Françoise Read is well known in the stamping world. She has been stamping for over ten years and designing stamps for the last six years. She currently has a license with Stampendous, an American stamp manufacturer. Prior to this she worked and designed for Funstamps in the UK. Francoise runs workshops for retailers and demonstrates at stamping shows around the country. Her work appears regularly in Crafts Beautiful and other craft publications. Francoise's can also be seen in Funstamps 'Beyond the Basics' video. She lives and works from home in Berkshire with her husband and son.

Dry embossing
Using a stencil embossing tool to draw and emboss patterns on the back of an image stamped on vellum.

Resist embossing
Stamping and embossing an image with a clear inkpad and powder. Sponging over the image with colour.

Brayering or using a roller
Applying ink from a dye based multicoloured inkpad to a large stamp or direct to paper.

Chalking
Stamping with a VersaMark inkpad and dusting coloured chalks over the image. The ink will pick up the chalk dust.

Tools

To complete the projects some of the following tools may be required:
- *Cutting mat, craft knife, metal ruler and scissors*
- *Novelty edge scissors*
- *Paper trimmer*
- *Sponge Daubers*
- *Fantastix or paintbrushes*
- *Rubber brayer*
- *Punches*
- *Dry embossing tool and foam mat*

Inks

Tsukineko manufactures all the inkpads used in the projects. All are acid-free and most are archival. It is important to use good products to achieve quality results. Here is a list of the various inks used in the projects:

VersaColor
Pigment ink suitable for general stamping. The ink is slow drying making it suitable for embossing. There is an excellent range of colours.

Emboss
The inkpads contain a clear or tinted ink. Stamp and emboss the image with clear or coloured embossing powders.

Encore Ultimate Metallic
A fast drying metallic pigment ink. Can also be embossed and looks great on light or dark card.

VersaMark
This ink gives a watermark effect. It is perfect for subtle tone-on-tone designs.

Fabrico
This craft ink can be used on lots of absorbent surfaces such as fabric, wood and shrink plastic. It is permanent once heat dried.

Kaleidacolor
Multicoloured dye based inkpads. The lovely colour combinations and unique sliding pad make these inkpads great to use.

Brilliance
Pigment inkpad that will dry on glossy surfaces such as vellum and metallic card. It is fast drying and comes in a beautiful range of pearlescent colours.

Materials

Stamping on a variety of surfaces gives you extra scope for creating. Here is a little information on some of the surfaces used in the projects:

Vellum Papers
Thin frosty transparent paper that looks very similar to tracing paper. It can vary in thickness and comes in a range of colours and pre- printed patterns. The smooth surface is excellent for stamping but be careful not to let your stamp slip or skid. Brilliance inkpads are ideal for this surface.

Perga Paper
A very thick version of vellum. It can withstand wetness so is ideal to create multicoloured backgrounds with a brayer and KaleidaColor inkpad.

Shrink Plastic
Comes smooth or pre-sanded. If smooth it must be sanded to give the ink a surface to key into. It is brittle so when cutting around an image a simple outline is best. It gives large stamps a new lease of life and you can create nice jewellery from it. Both Fabrico and Brilliance inkpads work well on shrink plastic.

Copper Foil
Thin metal gives a completely new look to

stamps. You can emboss on the line and use the image from the back or as in the Celtic Bird project you emboss on the sides of the line. The metal foil needs to be thin otherwise it is difficult to apply pressure and to draw small detail.

Adhesives

One of the questions most asked by stampers is "what glue do you use?" It is best to have several types of glue. I have the following at hand to use for my card making:

Xyron Machines
Xyron Machines are perhaps the most versatile and effective way of applying glue in most cases. They come in a variety of different sizes and can be fitted with cartridges that apply both re-positionable and permanent adhesives.

Spraymount Glue
A good alternative to a Xyron machine. Best used for layering. The strongest one is permanent. With this glue I know my samples will survive! However, it can be messy, and make sure you use it in a well ventalated area (not really suitable for children.)

Glue Stick
For gluing punched shapes or strips of vellum. Small items are best with this glue. Safe and easy to use. Ideal for children.

Hi-Tack Glue
When you are sticking bows, sequins and beads to add detail to your cards this glue is excellent. It is strong and dries clear.

Beaded Flowers

Create some exotic patterns with a simple flower motif. Simply stamp the motif and cut a basic stencil. Use the same colours for your stencilling and stamping and you will create beautiful background papers. String the flowers and add mini glass beads for texture. These will give the flowers a sparkly centre.

Required:	
STAMPS	MAGENTA - 23.085-G, 23.112-E.
INK	TSUKINEKO VERSACOLOR™ SINGLE-COLOR PADS; 24 OPERA PINK, 26 BOYSENBERRY, 36 HELIOTROPE.
CARD	SILVER, PALE PINK AND LILAC.
OTHER	PEARL BLUE EMBOSSING POWDER. LILAC PAPER CORD. TINY GLASS BEADS ⅛ AND ⅟₁₆ HOLE PUNCHES

6

1 Make a stencil for both flowers by stamping each one on scrap paper and cutting out the basic petal shape.

2 Take the large flower stencil and sponge flowers all over a piece of A5 pale pink card using the Opera pink and Heliotrope ink pads. Repeat process using the small flower stencil and Boysenberry ink pad.

3 Stamp some large flowers over the stencilled card using the Opera Pink ink pad. Try to stamp over the stencilled flowers of the same colour. Repeat process using the small flower stamp with the Boysenberry and Heliotrope ink pads.

4 Cut away a strip 1.5cm wide from the front panel of a folded silver card 10.5cm by 21cm. Trim a piece 6cm by 19.5cm from the stamped card.

Mount on a piece of lilac card 8cm by 20cm and stick to the front of the silver card.

5 Cut a strip 4cm by 21cm from the left over stamped card and stick it to the inside of the silver card on the back panel. On lilac card stamp and emboss three large flowers using the Boysenberry pad and pearl blue powder.

6 Cut out the flowers leaving a small border and punch a hole in two opposite petals with the 1/16 hole punch. Stick tiny glass beads in the centre of each flower.

7 Punch four holes through the front of the card, two in the top corner and two in the bottom corner of the stamped panel using the 1/8 punch. Thread the beaded flowers on a length of paper cord and thread both ends of the cord through the punched holes.

Tips

- Work on dark card with light coloured pads for a completely different look.
- Use a different flower stamp but the same stencil and stamp techniques.
- Thread beads to the cord as well as the flowers.

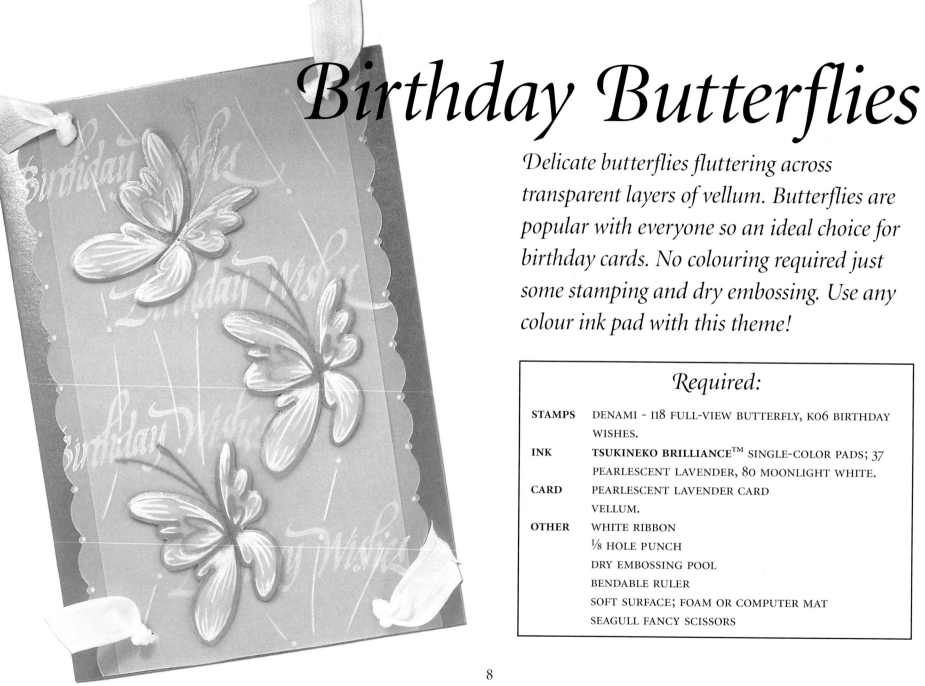

Birthday Butterflies

Delicate butterflies fluttering across transparent layers of vellum. Butterflies are popular with everyone so an ideal choice for birthday cards. No colouring required just some stamping and dry embossing. Use any colour ink pad with this theme!

Required:

STAMPS	DENAMI - 118 FULL-VIEW BUTTERFLY, K06 BIRTHDAY WISHES.
INK	TSUKINEKO BRILLIANCE™ SINGLE-COLOR PADS; 37 PEARLESCENT LAVENDER, 80 MOONLIGHT WHITE.
CARD	PEARLESCENT LAVENDER CARD VELLUM.
OTHER	WHITE RIBBON
	⅛ HOLE PUNCH
	DRY EMBOSSING POOL
	BENDABLE RULER
	SOFT SURFACE; FOAM OR COMPUTER MAT
	SEAGULL FANCY SCISSORS

1. On a piece of vellum, stamp three butterflies using the lavender ink pad. Allow ink to dry or use a heat gun. Turn the vellum over and place on a soft surface. Using the dry embossing tool draw lines within the butterfly wings to emphasise the shape.

2. Carefully cut out each butterfly leaving behind the antennae. Score the body of each butterfly and fold up the wings. On another piece of vellum 9cm by 17cm stamp three more butterflies using the lavender pad. Allow ink to dry or use a heat gun.

3. Turn vellum over and place on a soft surface. Use the dry embossing tool with the bendable ruler to draw some broken wavy lines between the butterflies. Draw some dots between the gaps in the lines.

4. Trim a piece of vellum 11cm by 17cm. Stamp the birthday wishes at random all over the vellum using the white ink pad. Allow ink to dry or use a heat gun. Cut the two side edges using the fancy scissors.

5. Turn the vellum over and place on a soft surface. Draw some dots below each little point using the dry embossing tool. Score and fold in half a piece of pearlescent lavender card 17cm by 24cm.

6. Layer the piece of vellum stamped with the butterflies on top of the larger piece of vellum stamped with the birthday wishes. Place both pieces on the front of the folded card and punch a hole through all the layers in each corner of the top sheet.

7. Thread white ribbon through the holes working from the back to the front. Tie a knot in the ends of the ribbon to secure the vellum to the card. Stick the folded butterflies over the stamped butterflies on the card and gently lift up the wings.

Tips

- ✌ Stamp the butterflies to go across the card instead of down.
- ✌ Work on coloured vellum instead of white.
- ✌ Try using different fancy scissors to cut the edges.

Bold Hearts

Arrange the hearts to suit and create maximum contrast by using strong colours against the black. Pre-cut foam shapes add texture and an element of fun! Scatter confetti to catch the light.

	Required:
STAMPS	DENAMI - J14 MED. BRUSHED HEART, N21 HEART BORDER.
INK	**TSUKINEKO VERSACOLOR**™ FIVE-COLOR PAD; 504 LOLLIPOP.
	TSUKINEKO VERSACOLOR™ SINGLE-COLOR PAD; 82 BLACK, 20 TURQUOISE.
	BLACK EMBOSSING POWDER.
CARD	WHITE, BLACK, SILVER AND YELLOW.
OTHER	PRE-CUT FOAM FLOWERS
	CONFETTI DOTS
	SPONGE DAUBERS

1. Cut a piece of white card 12cm square. Stamp and emboss four hearts using the black ink pad and black powder. Try to stack and overlap the hearts. Sponge ink over each of the hearts using four colours from the Lollipop pad.

2. Trim a piece of black card slightly larger than the white square and a piece of silver card slightly larger than the black card. Mount all the layers using spraymount glue on a 13.5cm square yellow folded card.

3. Stamp and emboss some small hearts on silver card using the black ink pad and black powder. Cut out the hearts and stick on the front of the card. Add the pre-cut foamflowers and a scattering of confetti dots to match the background colours.

Tips

- Use a different five-colour pad to change the sponged colour scheme.
- Another bold stamp can be used.
- Emboss the image in silver or gold to soften the look.
- Use other confetti shapes on the background.

Cave Painting

This project tries to reflect something of the period when an animal skin might have been one of the surfaces used by man to record his experiences. Use simple embellishments on the cards such as feathers, beads and twigs. Stamp with brown, red and black ink pads for earthy tones.

Required:

STAMPS	THE STAMP CONNECTION - D3010 SMALL BIRD IN FLIGHT, K3009 RUNNING SPEAR THROWER, D3003 SMALL LEFT FACING FERN.
INK	TSUKINEKO FABRICO™ SINGLE-COLOR PADS; 82 REAL BLACK, 152 SAND, AND 156 BRICK. TSUKINEKO BRILLIANCE™ SINGLE-COLOR PADS; 55 PEARLESCENT BEIGE, 94 COSMIC COPPER. ALL-PURPOSE INKS; 53 AUTUMN LEAF, 54 CHOCOLATE.
CARD	CREAM AND BLACK.
OTHER	CHAMOIS LEATHER, BROWN EMBROIDERY THREAD, 1/16 HOLE PUNCH, BEADS, FEATHERS.

1 On a 13cm square piece of chamois leather stamp several running spear throwers at random using the sand Fabrico™ ink pad. Stamp a single running spear thrower and bird in the centre of the square using the black Fabrico™ ink pad.

2 Stamp some fern leaves around the edges of the chamois leather square using the brick Fabrico™ ink pad. Paint patches of colour on the leather using the all-purpose inks. Allow the stamped leather to dry overnight before trimming it down into an irregular shape.

3 Cut a piece of black card 16cm square and stamp ferns at random all over the card using the pearlescent beige ink pad. Sponge copper ink over the edges of the stamped card.

4 Draw a 14cm square on the back of the stamped card leaving a one-centimetre border. Starting from one of the corners punch 28 holes two centimetres apart along the line of the drawn square.

5 Keeping the leather patch in the centre of the square take a needle and brown thread to attach and pull taunt the leather patch to the stamped card using the punched holes. Mount the completed cave painting on a folded cream card 17cm square.

6 Tie several lengths of brown thread in a knot around the front of the folded card. Thread some feathers through a round bead. Secure the bead to the feathers with glue. Tie the ends of the knotted thread around the ends of the feathers. Add some beads to the ends of the thread.

Tips

- Do not iron the Chamois leather as it shrinks.
- Stitch embellishments on the leather such as charms or beads.
- Stretch the leather across a frame made of sticks.

Celestial Sun & Moon

With these sparkly celestial cards, parts of the cards are cut away for a more unusual finish. There are all sorts of ways to fold or cut a card, so try something unusual and move away from the conventional. Glitter reminds us of the twinkling stars at night and the colours evoke the circle of night and day.

	Required:
STAMPS	FUNSTAMPS - F47 MOON & STARS, F46 SUN, A97 SWIRL, AA04 SOLID STAR.
INK	**TSUKINEKO VERSACOLOR**™ SINGLE-COLOR PADS; 13 ORANGE, 18 ROYAL BLUE, 19 CYAN, 31 APRICOT, 36 HELIOTROPE, 82 BLACK, 157 AMETHYST. **TSUKINEKO BRILLIANCE**™ SINGLE-COLOR PADS; 31 PEARLESCENT ORANGE, 37 PEARLESCENT LAVENDER. BLACK EMBOSSING POWDER.
CARD	WHITE, LILAC, YELLOW AND TURQUOISE BLUE.
OTHER	FINE GLITTER; RED, PURPLE AND BLUE. DOUBLE SIDED ADHESIVE SHEET. MINI STAR PUNCH.

1 Stamp and emboss both the sun and moon stamps on white card using the black ink pad and black powder. Colour both images before cutting them out.

2 Score and fold in half two pieces of turquoise blue card 11.5 cm by 23 cm to make two square cards. Sponge clouds across the front of both cards. Use the edge of some torn paper as a stencil and the royal blue and cyan ink pads.

3 On one of the cards stamp some swirls over the sponged clouds using the pearlescent lavender ink pad. Repeat process over the second card using stars instead of the swirls.

4 Stick the stamped sun in the middle of the card with the swirls. Draw a wavy diagonal line across the card to match up with the one behind the sun. Open the card flat and cut away the section above the sun and wavy diagonal line.

5 Stick the stamped moon in the middle of the card with the stars and repeat the cutting process above.

Stick glitter in selected areas around the sun and moon and over the wavy edges.

6 Cut two 11.5 cm squares, one out of yellow card and the other out of lilac card. Sponge clouds over both pieces of card using the edge of some torn paper as a stencil. Use the apricot and orange ink pads on the yellow card and the heliotrope and amethyst ink pads on the lilac card.

7 Stamp some swirls over the sponged clouds on the lilac card using the pearlescent lavender ink pad. Repeat process over the yellow card using stars and the pearlescent orange ink pad.

8 Stick the yellow piece inside the sun card on the back panel. Repeat process with the lilac piece and the moon card. Punch some mini stars out of a sheet of double sided adhesive. Stick them over the orange and purple clouds, peel away the top layer and add glitter.

Tips

- Work on dark card with light coloured inks for a different look.
- Colour the sun and moon images with emboss pens and use glitter embossing powder instead of glitter

Celtic Bird

Capture the appearance of a Celtic relic by stamping on metal. Embossing and ageing the metal makes the Celtic bird look as if it is an ancient artefact created centuries ago. Pick up the rich colours of the copper to complete the theme of the card.

	Required:
STAMPS	HERITAGE RUBBER STAMP CO - CELTSS4, CELTSS12, CELTL6, CELT3XLS7.
INKS	TSUKINEKO BRILLIANCE™ THREE-COLOR PAD; 05 TIRAMISU.
	TSUKINEKO BRILLIANCE™ SINGLE-COLOR PADS; 82 GRAPHITE BLACK, 31 PEARLESCENT ORANGE.
	CREAM LEATHER LOOK CARD.
CARD	BLACK AND DARK BROWN.
	CREAM MOUNTBOARD.
OTHER	0.003 MM COPPER FOIL.
	BLACK PLASTI-KOTE FAST DRY ENAMEL.
	DRY EMBOSSING TOOL.
	DECKLED EDGED SCISSORS.
	WIRE WOOL.

1 Sponge a piece of mountboard 8cm by 8cm with pearlescent orange ink. Stamp it over with the Celtic triangle using the brown ink. Smudge and soften the triangles with a sponge while the ink is wet. Stamp more Celtic triangles over the top of the mountboard using the pearlescent orange ink.

2 Stamp the Celtic bird twice on the copper foil using the black ink pad. Speed up drying by using a heat gun. Working on a soft surface, press down into the copper foil using the small point of the dry embossing tool. Outline the shapes within the bird. Add borders around both squares.

3 Paint both images with a thin coat of black 'plasti-kote' fast dry enamel. When dry rub off in patches using a small piece of wire wool to reveal the copper foil. The black enamel will have pooled in the recesses of the lines, making the image show up.

4 Cut out both squares using the deckled edged scissors. Age and colour the appearance of the

copper by holding it for a few seconds in an open flame. Glue one of the squares on the stamped mountboard.

5 Cut a piece of dark brown card 13cm by 13cm. Sponge beige and pearlescent orange and ink over the edge of some torn paper to create vertical and horizontal bands of colour across the card. Stamp spirals over the sponged card using the tiramisu ink pad. Mount on a slightly larger piece of black card.

6 Sponge pearlescent orange ink around the edges of a cream leather look card 15cm

square. Stamp Celtic circles over the edges, smudging them with a sponge for a softer effect. Stick the background in place on the card, adding the mountboard square. Tear off the corners of the remaining copper foil bird. Mould and glue them into place on the corners of the mountboard.

Tips

- ❧ Work on different coloured foils/metals.
- ❧ Use glass paint instead of the black enamel paint. It will need to dry for longer.
- ❧ Use a whole image to cover a piece of mountboard.

Chinese Lanterns

Follow the Chinese theme of the stamps by creating lantern shaped cards. Make the lanterns glow by using bright colours, sponging and translucent papers. Decorative flowers add the finishing touch.

Required:

STAMPS	MAGENTA - 23-329P, J-0286.
INK	**KALEIDACOLOR;** 09 BERRY BLAZE, 01 SPECTRUM.
	TSUKINEKO BRILLIANCE™ SINGLE-COLOR PAD; 82 GRAPHITE BLACK.
	TSUKINEKO VERSACOLOR™ SINGLE-COLOR PAD; 13 ORANGE, 17 VIOLET.
CARD	YELLOW, LILAC AND BLACK.
	ARTOZ PERGA PASTELL ; 211 WHITE.
OTHER	TASSELS, PAPER CORD.
	BRAYER.
	SPONGE DAUBERS.
	FANCY SCISSORS; DECKLED AND SEAGULL.
	FLOWER PUNCH, TINY DAISY PUNCH, 1/8 HOLE PUNCH.

1   Load the brayer with ink and roll evenly over a piece of Perga Pastell. A few layers of ink might be necessary for good coverage. Rotate the sheet to cover a large area and to avoid the colours mixing to browns. Use a heat gun to dry off the ink completely.

2   Using the black Brilliance™ pad stamp the Chinese grid on the Perga Pastell. Use the deckled edged scissors to cut out individual squares from the grid. Punch out the flowers and tiny daisies from the Perga Pastell.

3   Take a folded card 17cm square and draw the lantern shape on the card. Make sure to use the fold of the card as the base of the Lantern. Cut the sides of the lantern using the Seagull scissors. Cut away the neck of the lantern on the front piece of the card and cover the area left showing with black card.

4   Sponge ink over the edges of the lantern. Stamp dragonflies at random over the front of the lantern using the black Brilliance™ pad. Stick three squares in a column, slightly to one side on the card. Add the punched flowers to the lantern and a row of tiny daisies to the neck.

5   Punch a single hole in the base of the lantern. Thread the cord of the tassel through to the inside of the card. Cut the cord and glue the ends into the fold. Punch four holes in the neck of the lantern. Thread a length of cord through the holes to create a handle. Cut a little flap just below the neck of the lantern for closing purposes.

Tips

- Use the colours within the Kaleidacolor™ ink pad to influence the materials used to make the card.

- Change the shape of the card by using other oriental items such as a Kimono or fan.

Clowning Around

As an alternative to colouring why not try stamping on some colourful background papers. You can have fun selecting different outfits for your clown. Use up small pieces of paper and card to create patchworks backgrounds. Stitching is even easier when it is drawn!

Required:

STAMPS	FUNSTAMPS - F-R02 CLOWNING AROUND, F-R43 HAPPY BIRTHDAY BACKGROUND.
INK	**TSUKINEKO FABRICO**™ SINGLE-COLOR PAD; 82 BLACK. **TSUKINEKO VERSAMARK**™ WATERMARK/RESIST STAMP PAD.
CARD	WHITE, LILAC, LIME GREEN AND PALE YELLOW. SELECTION OF GINGHAM AND POLKADOT BACKGROUND PAPERS.
OTHER	PERMANENT BLACK FINE LINE PEN. HEART PUNCH - MINI BELLS. POMPOMS. - BUTTONS - EMBROIDERY THREAD.

1   *Stamp the clown on white card using the Fabrico™ ink pad. Use a heat gun to dry the ink and make it permanent. Colour in the face, fringe and bells.*

2   *Continue stamping the clown several times on the background papers and coloured card. Select one item of clothing from each clown and cut it out so that some of the outline is also trimmed. Arrange and stick down on the black and white clown.*

3   *Stitch some real bells onto the hat. Stick some real pompons onto the suit and the clown's hands and foot. Score and fold in half a piece of lime green card 14.5cm by 29cm.*

4   *Stamp the happy birthday background on some lilac card using the VersaMark™ pad. Cut out a small section of the stamped card and three other pieces from the background papers. Arrange the pieces on some white card. Make sure that the arrangement will fit on the folded card. Stick down the pieces.*

5   *Use the fine line pen to draw some stitching on the pieces for a quilt effect. Create two extra patches by drawing on the white card. Cut around the patches. Add some cross-stitch in one of the blank patches and stick some buttons in the other.*

6   *Mount the patchwork piece on the folded card and secure the clown in place using thick foam tabs. Stick three pompons above the clown and add some punched hearts to the lilac patch.*

Tips

❧   *Alter the colour scheme by using different background papers.*

❧   *Stamp the background papers should those that you have not be suitable.*

❧   *Use daisy shaped buttons instead of pompoms.*

21

Daisy Cat

Small is cute. These mini cards are sure to appeal to all animal lovers. This little cat is called Daisy so it seems only right to surround her with flowers. Make her stand out by using bright and cheerful background papers. A little bell on her collar makes her extra special!

Required:

STAMPS	HOBBY ART - QT420E MEDIUM DAISY, SC410F LARGE WINDOW.
INK	TSUKINEKO FABRICO™ SINGLE-COLOR PAD; 82 BLACK. TSUKINEKO VERSACOLOR™ SINGLE-COLOR PAD; 82 BLACK. EMBOSSING POWDERS; BLACK AND CLEAR. EMBOSS DUAL PENS.
CARD	WHITE, ORANGE, YELLOW AND PALE YELLOW. THIN NATURAL CORRUGATED CARD POLKA DOT BACKGROUND PAPERS; RED, BLUE, GREEN AND LIME GREEN.
OTHER	MEDIUM AND SMALL DAISY PUNCH - MINI CIRCLE PUNCH - JUMBO FLOWERPOT PUNCH - SHEER RIBBON TINY BELL.

Tips

❧ Colour in the cat or change it for a cute little dog.

❧ Add punched butterflies to flutter next to the flowers.

❧ Use soft pastel papers instead of bright colours.

❧ Use chalks to colour the cats for a softer effect.

1 On white card stamp and emboss three cats using the black pigment ink pad and black powder. Colour and emboss the noses and flowers on all three cats using emboss pens and clear powder. Cut out the cats leaving a tiny border.

2 On white card stamp three large windows using the black Fabrico™ ink pad. Cut away the top section of each window to leave the four panes and windowsill. Open up the windows by cutting away the panes.

3 Make three pairs of curtains from the red, blue and green background papers. Cut a square from each colour slightly smaller than the window and trim away two triangles. Stick the triangles to the back of the windows.

4 Cut and fold a piece of white card 10.5cm by 31.5cm into three equal sections. Trim three 9cm square pieces of lime green background paper. Stick the pieces to the panels on the folded card. Add a window to each panel.

5 Punch three flowerpots out of the corrugated card. Stick a flowerpot at the bottom of each window. Punch small and medium daisies from white, yellow and pale yellow card. Give all the daisies orange centres. Arrange and stick the daisies above each flowerpot.

6 Stick a cat next to each flowerpot. Thread some ribbon through the top of a tiny bell and tie into a bow. Stick the bell and bow below the flower ring on the first cat.

Gardening Apron

The relaxation of time spent tending the garden is the theme for this apron shaped card. Using collage allows you to make each new card slightly different from the last. Stamp mini tags to emphasise small details.

Required:	
STAMPS	STAMPENDOUS - XXSWS001 FRIENDSHIP GARDEN SET.
INK	TSUKINEKO VERSACOLOR™ SINGLE-COLOR PADS; 184 MISTY MAUVE, 187 SAGE
	TSUKINEKO ULTIMATE METALLIC FOUR-COLOR PAD; 401 ENCHANTED EVENING.
	TSUKINEKO FABRICO™ SINGLE-COLOR PAD; 82 BLACK
CARD	CREAM CARD.
VELLUM	PALE PINK AND PALE GREEN.
	THIN NATURAL CORRUGATED CARD.
OTHER	MINI TAGS.
	STRING.
	⅛ HOLE PUNCH AND LARGE FROG PUNCH.

1 Draw and cut out two curved lines down the sides of a cream card 11cm by 15cm to make an apron shaped card. Punch holes in the front of the card for the apron strings and neck loop.

2 Tear a piece of paper in half. Lay one of the torn edges across the front of the card at an angle and sponge some mauve ink across one side. Take the other torn piece of paper and repeat the process with the sage ink on the other side of the card.

3 Stamp the Friendship Garden across the card at random using the mauve ink. Stamp the flowerpot in the gaps using sage ink and the seed packet using the pink metallic ink. Tear small pieces of pale pink vellum and stick across the card.

4 On cream card stamp the Friendship Garden four times using the black Fabrico™ ink pad. Colour one whole image and only the pansies, leaves and snail out of the others. Sponge sage ink over the whole image before tearing out.

5 Draw a stitched outline around the whole image. Tear a square of pale green vellum. Stick the torn vellum on the card, adding the Friendship Garden patch. Make a pocket for the apron by cutting half a circle out of corrugated card. Glue in place.

6 Cut out the pansies and leaves. Stick to the apron using some foam tabs. Cut out the snail and stick to the bottom of the apron. Stamp the flower pot on a mini tag using the Fabrico™ ink pad and colour in. Use a foam tab to stick into place.

7 Use a Fabrico™ ink pad and the purple metallic ink to stamp out the wording. Sponge mauve and sage ink over the messages before tearing them out. Stick to the apron adding a layer of pale green vellum under the complete message. Punch a frog to add to the pocket of the apron. Thread string in holes to finish the apron

Tips

❧ Sew the patch to the card instead of drawing the stitches. Stamp on fabric for an authentic look

❧ Work from light to dark with your ink pads.

Gifts Galore

Using wrapping paper is great when you want to jazz up plain coloured cards! With so many brilliant patterns and textures available, the possibilities are endless. Go for a full glitter effect with sparkly embossing powders.

Required:

STAMPS	DENAMI; J18 SQUARE PRESENT, J36 SM. PRESENT, J19 STAR PRESENT, F116 STAR BALLOON.
INK	**TSUKINEKO VERSACOLOR**™ SINGLE-COLOR PAD; 82 BLACK. EMBOSSING POWDERS; BLACK AND HOLOGRAM. EMBOSS DUAL PENS.
CARD	WHITE CARD.
OTHER	22 GAUGE WIRE. CONFETTI DOTS AND FLOWERS. SHINY WRAPPING PAPER.

1 *On white card stamp and emboss all three presents and two balloons using the black ink pad and black powder. Colour and emboss the presents and balloons one at a time, using emboss pens and hologram powders. Cut out each item.*

2 *Cut and fold a piece of white card 18cm by 20.5cm. Spray glue all over one side of the card. Lay the card glue side down on a piece of wrapping paper slightly larger than the card. Smooth the wrapping paper down and trim off excess.*

3 *Working from the back stick the presents on the front of the card. By overlapping and using foam tabs, you can give the appearance that the presents are stacked.*

4 *Curl and twist two lengths of wire. Stick each wire to the back of a balloon. Use a foam tab to float the balloons above the presents. Add some confetti dots and flowers to come down the front of the card, around the presents and balloons.*

Tips

❧ *Use wallpapers to cover plain cards. An end of line roll is very cheap.*

❧ *Cut the wrapping paper in sections/strips to make the card multi-coloured.*

❧ *Stamp a silver outline for the presents and balloons for a softer look.*

Hug Me Teddy Blanket

Teddy bears are always popular and versatile. All the components are there within the set to mix and match. You can hang different items from the washing line to compliment your bears. Choose a colour scheme to please an adult or child.

	Required:
STAMPS	PSX - SK606 HUG ME TEDDY, F2320 BRUSHED HAPPY BIRTHDAY.
INK	**TSUKINEKO VERSACOLOR**™ SINGLE-COLOR PADS; 66 BURGUNDY
	TSUKINEKO FABRICO™ SINGLE-COLOR PAD; 82 BLACK.
	TSUKINEKO VERSAMARK™ WATERMARK/RESIST STAMP PAD.
	CLEAR EMBOSS PAD.
	EMBOSSING POWDERS; CLEAR AND PEARL BLUE.
CARD	CREAM, WHITE AND PALE BLUE.
OTHER	MINI WOODEN PEGS. - FINE PERMANENT BLACK PEN. SCALLOPED FANCY SCISSORS

1 On cream card, stamp and emboss footprint at random using the clear emboss pad and clear powder. Sponge burgundy ink in the gaps between the footprints.

2 Stamp more footprints in the gaps using the burgundy ink. Smudge the prints with a sponge for a softer effect. Clean off excess ink from the footprints with a soft tissue.

3 Draw a rectangle 9cm by 11cm on the back of the stamped card as a guide. Cut the blanket shape by turning the straight lines into soft wavy ones. Use the fancy scissors to trim the long edges of the blanket.

4 Cut some wavy strips out of cream card slightly longer then the blanket using the fancy scissors. Stick on them on the blanket trimming off the ends. Draw some stitching on the top and bottom ends of the blanket using the fine line pen.

5 Stamp two teddies on white card using the black Fabrico™ ink pad. Use a heat gun to dry the ink to make it permanent. Colour in the teddies in identical colours and cut them both out.

6 Score and fold a piece of cream card 24cm by 16.5cm. Cut a slightly smaller piece of pale blue card 11cm by 15.5cm. Stamp 'Happy Birthday' at random over the pale blue card using the VersaMark™ pad. Draw some stitching around the edges of the card using the fine line pen.

7 Mount the pale blue card on the folded cream card. Draw a washing line across the card using the fine line pen. Stamp and emboss 'Hug Me' on a small piece of cream card using the burgundy ink and pearl blue embossing powder. Tear out.

8 Stick the wooden pegs in place and hang the blanket, teddy and wording from the pegs. Use a foam tab to stick the second teddy at the bottom of the blanket.

Tips

❧ Change the pattern on the blanket by stamping 'Hug Me' instead of the footprint.

❧ Make the blanket out of fabric. Use a scrap of patterned fabric or stamp on some plain cotton.

Indian Spices

Stamp imaginary Indian silks richly woven with gold and silver threads on hand made papers. Combine your stamped papers with gold and silver card to keep the richness of the colours. Use simple geometrical shapes that are easy to cut and have fun creating different patterns.

Required:	
STAMPS	HERO ARTS - LL643 INDIAN.
INK	**TSUKINEKO ULTIMATE METALLIC** SOLID PAD; 10 GOLD, 12 SILVER.
CARD	A4 CARD; GOLD, SILVER, ORANGE AND TURQUOISE BLUE.
	A4 SHEETS OF THIN HANDMADE PAPERS; TEAL AND BRIGHT PINK.
OTHER	LARGE, MEDIUM AND TINY CIRCLE PUNCHES
	LARGE SUN PUNCH AND SQUIGGLE BORDER PUNCH.

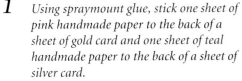

1 Using spraymount glue, stick one sheet of pink handmade paper to the back of a sheet of gold card and one sheet of teal handmade paper to the back of a sheet of silver card.

2 Make a template of a diamond by drawing two equilateral triangles side by side. The sides of both triangles should be 14cm long. Use the template to draw a diamond on both pieces of card.

3 Cut both diamonds, scoring and folding each one back into a single triangle. Cut two slightly smaller triangles to fit on the fronts of the triangular cards. One from orange card, the other from turquoise blue card. Select three stamps for each card.

4 Stamp a motif at random all over the orange triangle using the gold ink pad and mount on the gold folded card. Repeat process on the turquoise blue triangle using the silver pad and mount on the silver folded card.

5 Cut both a pink and a teal equilateral triangle with sides measuring 6.5cm out of the left over pieces from the card making. Stamp a motif at random in gold on the pink triangle and in silver on the teal triangle. Stick both triangles on the matching cards.

6 Punch three pink suns and three teal suns. Layer some circles punched out of the gold, silver, orange and turquoise blue card on each sun. Stick a sun in the middle of each of the outer triangles.

7 Create a triangular border on both cards by adding some punched squiggly lines. Use the two motifs left over to stamp a centrepiece for each card using the gold and silver pads on orange and turquoise blue card.

Tips

- Use other simple shapes such as a hexagon for your card.
- Follow other popular Indian colour combinations such as yellow, lime green and gold.
- Arrange left over pieces of stamped card into a patchwork to make up a simple card.

Let's Party

To celebrate in style why not go the whole way by making the invitations. You can choose a theme to match the decorations or the mood of the party. If you need to make quite a few, keep it simple by using multi-coloured ink pads, and for some dazzle – glitter embossing powder.

Required:	
STAMPS	RUBBER STAMPEDE - A2512D PARTY HAT, A2514D HAPPY CUPCAKE, A2515D BIRTHDAY SQUARE, A2471C LET'S PARTY!, A2405C PARTY BALLOON, A2445C FUNFETTI.
INK	**TSUKINEKO VERSACOLOR™ FIVE-COLOR PAD; 502 PASSION FRUIT.** GLITTER EMBOSSING POWDER.
CARD	MANGO, LIME GREEN, SEA GREEN. WHITE PERGA PASTELL.
OTHER	¼ RECTANGLE HAND PUNCH. SHEER RIBBON; PINK AND LILAC WAVE FANCY SCISSORS.

1   Cut three pieces of white Perga Pastell 11cm square. On each piece stamp and emboss a different image at random using the Passion Fruit Pad and glitter powder. Use the Funfetti, Party Balloon and Let's Party stamps.

2   To one side of each piece cut a window 4.5cm by 5cm. Leave a side border 2cm wide and top and bottom borders 3cm wide.

3   Cut a piece of card 11cm by 14.5cm from all three colours. Score and fold a flap 3.5cm wide on each piece. Trim the edge of each flap using the fancy scissors.

4   Punch two holes in each flap. Slip one stamped piece under each flap and mark out the holes. Remove the stamped pieces and punch the holes. Stick the stamped pieces to the flaps making sure to match up the holes.

5   Holding down the front of the card, carefully stamp an image in each window. Loop a length of ribbon through the holes in each card. Trim the ribbons to match.

Tips

- Use pearl blue embossing powder for a more subtle effect.
- For a classic look keep to white and silver colour scheme.
- Short of time? Then leave out cutting the window but stamp on the flap instead.

Mackintosh Round

Try making a special central piece for a card using a modelling compound. By stamping into the surface the image changes its appearance because it is in relief and no longer flat. Dusting the surface of the tile with Pearl-Ex will make it look metallic, giving it a real Mackintosh mark.

	Required:
STAMPS	HERITAGE RUBBER STAMP CO - MA2XLS2, MAXLS6.
INK	TSUKINEKO BRILLIANCE™ SINGLE-COLOR PADS; 36 PEARLESCENT PURPLE, 92 PLATINUM PLANET.
CARD	SILVER, BLACK AND LILAC.
	SILVER SCULPEY III MODELLING COMPOUND.
	PEARL-EX; 684 FLAMINGO PINK, 686 TURQUOISE AND 688 MISTY LAVENDER.
OTHER	PASTA MACHINE OR ROLLING PIN.
	SMALL SQUARE PUNCH.
	LARGE SOFT MAKEUP BRUSH

1 Use a pasta machine or a rolling pin to roll out a 3mm thick piece of silver modelling compound large enough to fit the Mackintosh motif. Stamp the motif into the modelling compound and if necessary reduce the size of the tile.

2 Dust the surface of the stamped tile with the Pearl-Ex colours using the soft makeup brush. Bake the tile in a normal oven following the instructions on the packet.

3 Cut a piece of black card 10cm by 14.5cm. Sponge pearlescent purple ink over the edge of some torn paper to create vertical and horizontal bands of colour across the card.

4 Stamp the Mackintosh flower stem several times over the edges of the black card using the pearlescent purple ink pad. Punch a square into some paper to make a stencil. Use platinum ink to stencil squares at random on the black card.

5 Punch squares out of the black card before mounting it on a slightly larger piece of silver card. Trim the silver card to leave only the two side borders. Punch further squares into the black card.

6 Score and fold in half a piece of lilac card 24cm by 14.5cm. Mount the completed background piece on the front of the folded card. Stick the tile on the front of the card with some strong glue.

Tips

❧ Make holes in the tile and secure to the card with ribbon.

❧ Use a pastry cutter to make different shaped tiles.

❧ Stamp the motif on a mountboard tile instead of the modelling compound.

Nautical Collage

Creating a collage is not difficult if you follow the simple step of trying out and arranging all the necessary items on your card before sticking them down. It is also quite satisfying to be able to recycle postage stamps or to use shells you have collected whilst on holiday.

Required:	
STAMPS	STAMPENDOUS - XXP003 LIGHTHOUSE COLLAGE.
INK	TSUKINEKO BRILLIANCE™ SINGLE-COLOR PAD; 18 MEDITERRANEAN BLUE.
	FROSTED SHRINK PLASTIC.
	THIN WATERCOLOUR PAPER.
CARD	BLUE, RED, GREEN AND WHITE.
OTHER	POSTAGE STAMPS.
	SHELLS.
	STRING.
	TINY COMPASS

1 On watercolour paper stamp the lighthouse collage using the blue Brilliance™ pad. Before the ink dries completely apply thin washes of clear water over the image to make the blue lines bleed.

2 Add highlights of colour to the image using pens and thin washes of water. Before tearing out the image sponge blue ink around the lighthouse, flags, rope and compass.

3 Stamp the lighthouse collage twice on a piece of frosted shrink plastic using the blue Brilliance™ ink pad. Allow both to dry before cutting out one complete image and only a section of the other. Shrink using a heat gun or normal oven. Keep heating the plastic until it has curled and flattened back out.

4 Cut a piece of blue card 10cm by 14cm and stamp the lighthouse collage at random all over the card using the blue Brilliance™ ink pad. Stick some small torn pieces of green card and postage stamps on the stamped card. Trim down any over hanging pieces.

5 Stick the torn watercolour image so that it overlaps the postage stamps and green card on the stamped card. Arrange the pieces of shrink plastic, compass, shells and knotted string around the watercolour image and stick into place.

6 Mount the completed collage on a slightly larger piece of white card. Repeat layering process on a slightly larger piece of red card. Take a folded white card 12.5cm by 16.5cm and stick the layered collage to the card.

Tips

- Use a different theme such as a fishing or golf for the collage.
- Start a collection of little items suitable for collages.
- Use a limited number of colours when stamping and adding highlights so that the collage does not look too busy and overcrowded.

Pansies

Although the stamped flowers on this card are bold, by using a layer of vellum it is like seeing the flowers through frosted glass. Small stamps that are easy to cut out and colour are highly versatile. You can arrange the flower heads into rows, columns and rings. Thin vellum can be layered up over card without creating too much bulk.

Required:

STAMPS	PSX - C2506 BRUSHED PANSY, C2509 WITH LOVE.
INK	**TSUKINEKO BRILLIANCE**™ SINGLE-COLOR PAD; 80 MOONLIGHT WHITE.
	TSUKINEKO VERSACOLOR™ SINGLE-COLOR PAD; 82 BLACK.
	PEARL BLUE EMBOSSING POWDER.
	ALL-PURPOSE INKS; 36 WISTERIA, 11 LEMON YELLOW.
CARD	WHITE CARD.
	PEARLESCENT LILAC PAPER.
	PSX PURE WHITE VELLUM PAPER.
OTHER	¹⁄₁₆ HOLE PUNCH.
	3MM SILK RIBBON.

1 On white card stamp and emboss four pansies using the black ink pad and pearl blue embossing powder. Paint the pansies using the all-purpose inks and cut out the flower heads.

2 Cut and fold a piece of white card 14cm by 31.5cm into three equal sections. Trim away a 5cm section from the right hand panel. Spray glue all over the back of the left-hand panel and cover with pearlescent lilac paper.

3 Cut and score a piece of white vellum paper 14cm by 31.5cm into three equal sections. Trim away a 5cm section from the right hand panel.

4 Cover the middle panel of the vellum and using the white Brilliance™ ink pad stamp 'With Love' on the right-hand panel and pansies on the left-hand panel. Fold up the vellum so that the stamped panels are on the outside. Cut two small slots in the middle of the centre panel.

5 Stick the stamped pansies in a column down the right hand panel of the folded white card. Wrap the card up in the stamped vellum and punch a single hole through both layers in the left-hand and right-hand side corners of the side panels.

6 Cut two lengths of ribbon long enough to link up the holes on each side panel. Thread the ribbon through the holes working from the back to the front and secure with knots.

7 Thread a length of ribbon through the slots at the back of the card. Bring the ends of the ribbon round to the front of the folded card and secure the card closed by tying the ends into a bow.

Tips

- Use a different flower head, like a Daisy.
- Try changing the colours of the pansies or ink pad.
- Use layers of coloured vellum and change the colour of the ribbon.

Patchwork Pears & Dragonflies

With enamelling and random stamping no two cards look the same, so you can make the motifs in these cards look different each time. Use some glitter embossing powders to add a sparkle to your tiles. If you do not like the result melt it back down and re-stamp.

Required:	
STAMPS	RUBBER STAMPEDE - A2380E WHIMSICAL PEAR, A2379E WHIMSICAL DRAGONFLY.
INK	**TSUKINEKO VERSACOLOR**™ SINGLE-COLOR PADS; 131 NARCISSUS, 133 SEASHELL, AND 136 BABY BLUE. **TSUKINEKO ULTIMATE METALLIC** FOUR-COLOR PAD; 402 SWEET DREAMS. **TSUKINEKO ULTIMATE METALLIC** SINGLE-COLOR PAD; 06 BLUE. CLEAR EMBOSS PAD - EMBOSSING POWDERS; CLEAR, PEARL BLUE, ROSE QUARTZ - CLEAR ENAMELLING POWDER - MOUNTBOARD
CARD	CREAM AND PALE BLUE.
OTHER	3 MM PINK RIBBON.

1 Cut two 12cm squares, one out of cream card and the other out of blue card. On the cream square stamp and emboss pears at random using the clear emboss pad and clear powder. Repeat process on the pale blue card using dragonflies.

2 Sponge seashell, baby blue and narcissus ink over both the squares. Remove excess ink from the embossed areas with a soft tissue. Cut up each piece of card into nine equal squares.

3 Cut two 12.5cm squares, one out of cream card and the other out of blue card. Arrange and stick down nine squares of alternating colour on both larger pieces of card. Leave a tiny border of card showing all around.

4 Score and fold into half a piece of cream card 15cm by 30cm. Make a second card the same size out of pale blue card. Mount each patchwork square onto a card. Stick three lengths of ribbon across both cards.

5 Cut two pieces of mountboard 4cm by 8cm. Ink up one of the pieces with blue metallic ink. Dip the whole piece into the enamelling powder and shake off the excess powder. Heat and melt the powder. Repeat this process 3 to 4 times.

6 Sprinkle some pearl blue and rose quartz embossing powders on top of the final layer whilst it is still hot. Use the sweet dreams pad to ink up the pear.

7 Re-heat the surface of the melted enamel powder and stamp the pear into the hot surface. Wait a few seconds before lifting the stamp. Repeat the process for the dragonfly tile. Stick a tile to each card on top of the ribbons.

Tips

- Cut your mountboard to a different size and shape.
- Instead of sponging, try to ink over the stamped pears and dragonflies, stamping them directly in colour.
- Try a different patchwork pattern by looking at some quilting books.

Perfume Bottle

On this card the chalks are used to colour the line, but also work effectively to colour the background in soft, muted tones. The image of the perfume bottle and pearls remind us of items found on an old fashioned dressing table next to a jewellery box and mirror.

Required:	
STAMPS	STAMPENDOUS - XXL005 DAISY BORDER, XXW002 EAU DE PARFUM.
INK	**TSUKINEKO VERSAMARK**™ WATERMARK/RESIST STAMP PAD.
CARD	WHITE AND SEA GREEN CARD.
OTHER	DECORATING CHALKS OR CHALK PASTELS. COTTON WOOL AND COTTON BUDS. THIN SHEER RIBBON. STRING OF SMALL BEADS.

beads as white as possible and use the cotton buds to pick up small detail.

3 Trim down the stamped image into a square approximately 9cm by 9cm. Mount on a slightly larger piece of sea green card.

1 On white card stamp the perfume bottle using the VersaMark™ pad. Take a small piece of cotton wool and gently dust pale pink chalk over the whole image to make the stamped area more visible.

2 Build up the colours over the bottle, brooch and tassels, dusting in patches with turquoise green, bright pink and petrol blue chalks. Try to emphasise the shape of the bottle and brooch. Try to keep the pearl

4 On a folded white card 15cm square stamp a daisy border down both sides of the card using the VersaMark™ pad. Dust both borders in the same colours as the main image.

5 Mount the perfume bottle on the front of the stamped card at an angle to overlap the daisy borders. Tie a bow out of sheer ribbon around a small string of beads and stick to the card.

Tips

- ❧ Restrict the number of colours used to three or four that blend well together.
- ❧ Add embellishments to the card similar to those portrayed on the stamp such as lace and charms.
- ❧ For a richer look stamp and emboss the image using a gold pigment ink pad and gold powder before adding colour.

Pressed Flowers

Bring the beauty of the garden into your home by creating delicate flower collages. The chalks give the cards a soft, muted appearance. The netting is almost transparent, resembling dew on a spider's web.

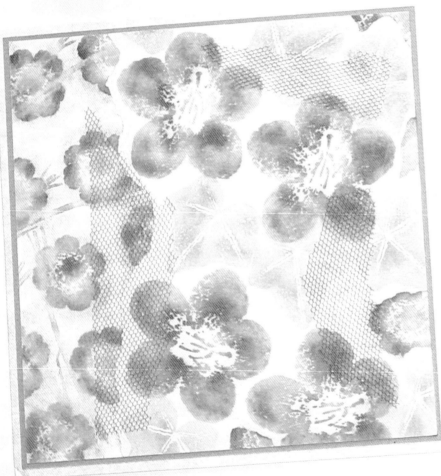

<table>
<tr><td></td><td>Required:</td></tr>
<tr><td>STAMPS</td><td>RUBBER STAMPEDE- 2877B COSMOS BLOSSOM, 2867H GERBERA DAISY, 2876F WILD GRASS, 2873E DAISY STEM, 2866C GERANIUM LEAF.</td></tr>
<tr><td>INK</td><td>TSUKINEKO VERSAMARK™ WATERMARK/RESIST STAMP PAD.</td></tr>
<tr><td>CARD</td><td>CREAM AND PASTEL GREEN.</td></tr>
<tr><td>OTHER</td><td>DECORATING CHALKS OR CHALK PASTELS. COTTON WOOL AND COTTON BUDS. FINE ORANGE NETTING.</td></tr>
</table>

1   On cream card start by stamping a couple of Gerbera daisies leaving only a small gap between them using the VersaMark™ pad. Take a small piece of cotton wool and gently dust pale yellow chalk over the flowers. Keep repeating this process until you have stamped and dusted approximately six Gerbera Daisies.

2   Build up the colours over the flowers, dusting in patches with pale orange, bright orange and red chalks. Try to emphasise the petals and centre of the flowers. Stamp some Wild grass between the Gerbera Daisies using the VersaMark™ pad. Dust over the grass using two shades of green. Tear out a section of the panel and some smaller pieces.

3   Stamp and dust a row of Cosmos Blossoms using the same process but using yellow chalk for the centre of the flower and pinks and purples for the petals. Tear out part of the row. Stamp and dust a small panel of Geranium leaves using two shades of green and tear out a section.

4   Trim a piece of cream card 12cm by 15cm. Stamp a column of Daisy stems on the right hand side of the card using the VersaMark™ pad. Dust the flowers in yellow and pinks and the stems in pale green.

5   Take all the stamped flower pieces and arrange on the stamped cream card. Tear or cut small sections of netting. Add some netting between the card layers and on the front of the pieces.

6   Stick arrangement down on the cream card using spraymount glue. Trim down any bits that go over the edge of the card. Trim a piece of pastel green card slightly larger than the flower panel. Stick both pieces on a folded cream card 13.5cm by 16.5cm.

Tips

- Use felt tips directly on the stamps. Stamp on scrap paper first to give a softer look.
- Use fading technique to stamp a flower border
- Try working on soft, pastel coloured card. A soft lilac will enhance pink flowers and a soft apricot works well with orange flowers.

Rose Garden

Keep to a simple colour scheme but achieve depth with the layers of card, mountboard and tissue paper. The roses and butterflies become one in this poetic garden.

	Required:
STAMPS	HERO ARTS- LL561 GARDEN WOODCUTS, S1832 ITALIAN POETRY BACKGROUND.
INK	TSUKINEKO BRILLIANCE™ SINGLE-COLOR PAD; 21 GAMMA GREEN, 80 MOONLIGHT WHITE.
CARD	WHITE AND GOLD. WHITE MOUNTBOARD.
OTHER	ARTOZ PERGA PASTELL; 339 FIRTREE GREEN. PALE GREEN TISSUE PAPER. ⅛ HOLE PUNCH AND LARGE BUTTERFLY PUNCH. 3MM GOLD RIBBON

1 Cut a 5.5cm by 5.5cm square of mountboard. Stamp the roses using the green Brilliance™ ink pad on the square. Lightly sponge green ink over the roses allowing some of the background to show through. Apply deeper layers of ink on the edge and border around the roses.

2 Stamp script background on white card using green Brilliance™ ink pad. Tear out and sponge the edges of the card with green ink. Take a sheet of pale green tissue paper and stamp rows of roses. Tear into small sections

3 Cut a long piece of green Perga Pastell 8.5cm by 17cm. Stamp roses at random all over the Perga Pastell using the white Brilliance™ ink pad. Trim a piece of gold card slightly larger than the stamped piece. Mount the stamped piece on the gold card using spraymount glue.

4 Punch holes down the side of a folded white card 12cm by 20cm, at equal intervals. Thread gold ribbon through the holes working from back to front, up and back down. Tie ends of the ribbon into a knot.

5 Take all the stamped pieces and mount on the card, building up the layers so that the tissue paper sections are applied last covering part of the mountboard. Stamp some roses on white card using the green

Brilliance™ ink. Sponge lightly over the roses with the green ink.

6 Punch gold butterflies and stick them to the front of the card. Punch the same quantity of butterflies from the stamped roses. Score the wings and fold. Stick the green rose butterflies directly on top of the gold butterflies.

Tips

- ❧ Use a different colour to influence the overall colour scheme.
- ❧ Use pre-printed background papers if you have no suitable stamp.
- ❧ Build the card up using a different stamp from the set.

Stone Etchings

Catch the sun and watch the reflections appear behind the stone etchings. Adding the mesh pieces gives the stone textures a modern feel. Include a frame as a gift with your card to turn your masterpiece into an elegant addition to any room.

Required:

STAMPS	HERO ARTS - LL636 STONE ETCHINGS, LL648 STONE BORDERS, S1832 ITALIAN POETRY BACKGROUND.
INK	**TSUKINEKO BRILLIANCE™** SINGLE-COLOR PADS; 80 MOONLIGHT WHITE, 82 GRAPHITE BLACK.
CARD	BLACK, SILVER, WHITE AND GREY.
OTHER	SILVER MESH
	OLD CDS

1 On white card stamp several stone etchings using the black ink pad. Cut a circular design in half and tear two other designs leaving only sections of the stamped image.

2 Stamp several stone borders on the blank side of a CD using the black ink pad. Use a heat gun to quicken the drying process. Score sections of the CD with a craft knife and carefully snap into pieces.

3 On a piece of black card 9cm by 10cm stamp the Italian poetry background using the white ink pad. Score and fold in half a piece of card 14cm by 25cm. Trim a slightly smaller piece of silver card to mount on the front of the folded card.

4 Stick the sections of the stone etchings on the stamped poetry background. Cut irregular pieces out of the silver mesh, and stick to overlap on top of some of the stone etchings.

5 Trim a piece of grey card slightly larger then the black card and a piece of white card slightly larger then the grey card. Mount the black card on the grey card and layer onto the white card. Stick in place on the silver card.

6 Stick the stamped CD pieces on the front of the card and add a piece of silver mesh in the bottom right hand corner.

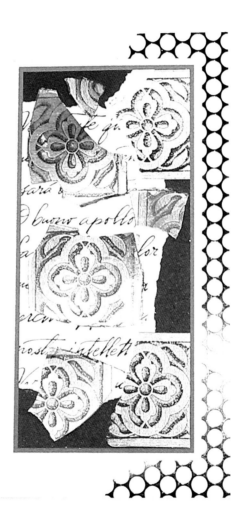

Tips

- Use a different range of colours to influence the overall colour scheme such as blues and purples.
- Use the mesh as a stencil to sponge a background.
- Achieve a mosaic effect by using the CD pieces to create a simple shape.

Tumbling Bears & Presents

Have fun with shrink plastic and a cuddly bear bearing gifts. Bright coloured card, inkpads and ribbon are combined with some simple mounting to create a great birthday card.

Required:	
STAMPS	HOBBY ART – BEARING GIFTS LT10F, HAPPY BIRTHDAY BACKGROUND GR732E.
INK	**TSUKINEKO FABRICO**™ SINGLE-COLOR PAD; 82 BLACK. **TSUKINEKO VERSACOLOR**™ SINGLE-COLOR PADS; 14 SCARLET, 17 VIOLET, 22 FRESH GREEN.
CARD	WHITE, RED, GREEN, PURPLE AND YELLOW
OTHER	WHITE SHRINK PLASTIC. CLEAR EMBOSSING POWDER. COLOURING PENCILS. STAR PUNCH AND TINY STAR PUNCH. 7 MM AND 3 MM SILK RIBBON; RED, GREEN & PURPLE

1 Using the black Fabrico™ pad, stamp 3 bears on the rough side of a pre-sanded sheet of white shrink plastic. Allow to dry before colouring each bear with pencils.

2 Punch a hole in a scrap piece of card and use it to draw a circle above each bear's head. Cut out each bear leaving a 3mm border. Punch out the circle. Shrink the bears using a heat gun or normal oven. Keep heating the plastic until it has curled and flattened back out.

3 On white card stamp the 'Happy Birthday' background 3 times using each of the VersaColor™ pads and emboss with clear powder. Trim each background down to the same size.

4 Back each piece with the appropriate coloured card and trim to leave a 2mm border. Stick two length of matching 3mm ribbon in a cross on each piece with fabric glue.

5 Thread a small length of 3mm ribbon through the hole in each bear. Using fabric glue attach one bear to each present. Tie a bow of each colour in the 7mm ribbon and stick them in place, one to the top of each present.

6 Score and fold a piece of white card 10 cm by 20cm and stick the presents at angles going down the card. Start with the top present and overlap each one. Add some punched stars around the presents.

Tips

❧ If your pad is very wet, stamp off excess ink on some scrap paper before stamping onto plastic.

❧ Apply colours lightly as they will intensify when the plastic shrinks.

❧ Use the wood block of a stamp to flatten plastic when it has finished shrinking.

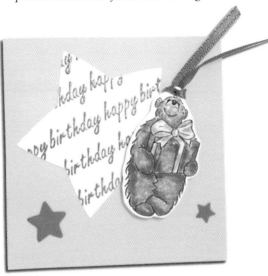

Variations

❧ Use different coloured pads and card.

❧ Emboss with Glitter powder or Pearl Blue to achieve different backgrounds.

❧ Replace white shrink plastic with frosted shrink plastic.

Under the Sea

Clear layers of enamel powder are like clear glass – so perfect for a water theme. The four fish make a stunning motif that can be used on its own or to stamp a pattern. It could represent a star sign or a person's involvement with the sea and diving. The fish is also a Christian symbol.

Required:

STAMPS	THE STAMP CONNECTION - BIJOUX COLLECTION J7241 GOLDFISH, J7031 LARGE SEAWEED, A7027 BUBBLES.
INK	TSUKINEKO BRILLIANCE™ SINGLE-COLOR PAD; 18 MEDITERRANEAN BLUE.
	TSUKINEKO VERSACOLOR™ SINGLE-COLOR PAD; 42 LIME, 158 LAPISLAZULI.
	CLEAR EMBOSS PAD.
	CLEAR ENAMEL POWDER.
	LIME GREEN GLITTER EMBOSSING POWDER.
CARD	ROYAL BLUE, LIME GREEN AND CORNFLOWER BLUE.
	WHITE MOUNTBOARD.
OTHER	LIME GREEN GAUGE RIBBON.

1 Cut an 8cm square of mountboard. Sponge lime and lapislazuli ink all over the mountboard square. Stamp the goldfish on the mountboard using the blue Brilliance™ ink pad. Using a craft knife with a sharp blade cut out the goldfish. Sponge the edge of the mountboard with lime and lapislazuli ink.

2 Press the stamped side of the mountboard on a clear emboss pad. Dip the whole piece into the enamelling powder and shake off the excess powder. Heat and melt the powder. Repeat this process a second time. Sprinkle a tiny amount of lime green glitter embossing powder while the surface is still hot.

3 Score and fold into half a piece of lime green card 14cm by 28cm. Trim a 12.5cm square of royal blue card. Mount on the folded card.

4 Trim an 11cm square of cornflower blue card and an 11.7cm square of lime green card. Using the blue Brilliance™ pad stamp seaweed on all four corners of the blue square. Stamp bubbles over the edges of the lime green square. Mount both pieces on the royal blue square.

5 Trim an 8cm square of cornflower blue card and an 8.7cm square of lime green card. Using the blue Brilliance™ pad stamp bubbles all over the blue square but only over the edges of the lime green square. Layer both pieces at an angle on the folded card.

6 Stick the goldfish on top of the last square. Tie a knot in a small piece of the gauge ribbon and fray the ends. Glue the knot in place on one of the corners of the card.

Tips

- Use yellow, orange and red ink pads for a tropical look.
- Decorate the card with small shells.
- Stick strips of the gauge ribbon across the card to create a fishing net.

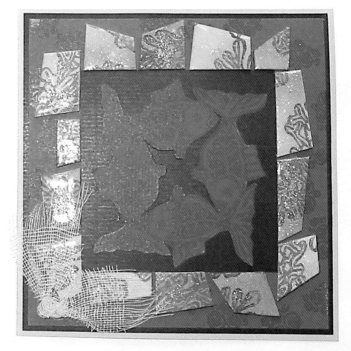

Watercolour Iris

Imagine being caught in the rain whilst outside painting a watercolour. The image is dotted with raindrops and it slowly fades, the colours mixing. Stamp on watercolour paper to use this idea in the comfort of your home. Always remember your basic colour mixing when choosing which colours to blend and mix.

Required:	
STAMPS	PSX - K3131 IRIS RENAISSANCE BOTANICAL
INK	**TSUKINEKO KALEIDACOLOR**™ STAMP PAD; 21 RIVIERA.
	FABRICO SINGLE-COLOR PAD; 82 REAL BLACK
CARD	YELLOW, GREEN AND WHITE.
	THIN WATERCOLOUR PAPER.
OTHER	BRAYER

Kaleidacolor™

RAISED RAINBOW DYE INKPAD

RIVIERA

1 Place the Iris stamp rubber side up on a flat surface. Load the brayer with ink from the Kaleidacolor™ pad and roll evenly over the stamp several times. Stamp the iris on a piece of watercolour paper.

2 Carefully apply thin layers of water at random over the iris to make the inks bleed. Work in one colour area at a time to avoid over mixing the inks. The aim is to soften parts of the iris whilst retaining clear areas.

3 Trim down the image to remove the border. On white card, stamp the iris using the black Fabrico™ ink pad. Heat set the ink before colouring the image. Tear the stamped card into little sections.

4 Arrange some of the torn sections over the watercolour iris so that they match up. Allow the watercolour

iris to show through by leaving gaps. Stick the pieces down and trim any that overhang over the edges.

5 Layer the watercolour iris on some green card and yellow card. Trim both pieces to leave a small border. On a folded white card 13cm by 17cm, stamp two irises going across the card at different angles using the brayer and Kaleidacolor™ pad.

6 Tear two corner pieces from a piece of green card and stick over the opposite

corners of the folded card. Mount the watercolour iris on the card to one side so that some of the stamped background is visible.

Tips

- ❧ Achieve a completely different mood by using another Kaleidacolor™ pad.
- ❧ Brayer a section of the folded card to create another background.
- ❧ Cut out sections of a stamped image instead of tearing.